BUILDING A
SUPERNATURAL CHURCH

Mark T. Barclay

All scripture references are quoted from the
King James Version of the Holy Bible
unless otherwise noted.

Third Printing 1997

ISBN 0-944802-11-7

Write:
Mark Barclay Ministries
P.O. Box 588, Midland, MI 48640-0588

CONTENTS

A WORD FROM THE AUTHOR

I have noticed that churches and pastors all over the world are struggling to start and develop supernatural churches and fellowships.

It is easy to see that no one, as yet, has **all** the perfect knowledge and wisdom needed to complete this task. However, God has given wisdom to some and Bible revelation to others on how to **do the work** pastoring successfully.

I have written this small handbook of guidelines to help pastors better equip themselves and the church. Why? Because we are entering the most strategic time of spiritual warfare ever. The Lord is soon to return, and we must have our work done and be in the condition He wishes, full of faith, spotless and without blemish.

Please allow the Lord to expand your vision and knowledge as you look into this book. My prayer for you is that God will use these few pages of instructions and examples to bless your church and enrich your experience of pastoring.

CHAPTER 1
THE CHURCH

In the late part of 1979, God began to deal with me about pastoring His people. Up to this time I was traveling, teaching in other fellowships, and really wondering what my call was. Oh yes, I was successful at evangelistic work, but I wasn't satisfied. As I submitted my heart and life more and more to the Lord, He began to draw me with His sweet Spirit into the office to which He had called me. What a privilege to be used of the Lord in this hour of human history.

As I sought the Lord, He began to show me more and more about His Church and how the local fellowships (churches) of believers were to be organized, disciplined, and unified. Following are the four aspects of the local church that He revealed to me:

1. AN OASIS OF LOVE

The Bible says they will know us by our love (John 13:34-35). Humanity is very sad today. People are sick, rejected, deprived, poor, discouraged, and lost. They need and desire a refuge of protection, a place they can run to and be freed, protected, fed, and accepted. The local church should be just that—a gathering of God's people who

1

understand, forgive, love, and accept.

In the local church that I pastor, we are working hard at loving each other and accepting those who come in. We know that love never fails and that perfect love casts out all fear. We want to love all people into God's Kingdom. This means we are asking God to send us sinners, prostitutes, drug addicts, alcoholics, rich men, poor men, and all others who need love, attention, and a living Christ. We want them to come into this oasis and be refreshed and rescued in that love.

2. A CHRIST-GOVERNED WORD CHURCH

According to the Bible, Jesus is the Head of the Church (Eph. 5:23). He has designed the Church in a special order so that He may give commands or directions, through His Word or His Spirit, and be assured that these orders will reach His people. Jesus really doesn't care what your opinion is, nor mine. He simply decrees what He wants, and it's up to us to hear and carry it out. I will write more about this in the chapter called "Governments."

What is a Word church? It is a local church that establishes its doctrines and regulations from the Bible rather than the traditions of men.

People are tired of churches falling apart, leaders falling into sin, and elder or deacon boards ruling instead of Christ. Jesus is the Head of the Church, the Holy Spirit is His representative here, and the pastor is His under-shepherd.

Where the Spirit of the Lord is there is liberty (2 Cor. 3:17), but things must be done decently and in order (1 Cor. 14:40).

3. A BELIEVERS' BIBLE TRAINING CENTER

Every believer needs Bible training and teaching with a place to practice what they have learned. The church should be this place. Jesus gave gifts to men (Eph. 4:8-11), and these gifts are given to train His people to do the work of the ministry (Eph. 4:12-13). The Bible shows us that without knowledge we are easily destroyed (Hos. 4:6), and Paul also wrote and said that he would not want the brethren to be ignorant (1 Cor. 12:1).

The church should be a training ground, not just a teaching center. Bible teaching is very important, but specialized training is mandatory if people are going to be expert doers of the Word they hear.

4. AN EVANGELISTIC OUTREACH CENTER

We all want to reach people for Jesus. It is harvest-time, and the fields are white and ready. We have been commissioned to go into all the world and preach the gospel to every creature (Matt. 28:18-20). How? By trained believers in the community going to families, schools, and businesses; missionaries going to other countries; elders going to the hospitals, widows, fatherless, jails, and convalescent homes. By all of these people going about doing good and witnessing of what great things the Lord has done for them.

Just what are we saying the Church is then? Those called-out ones. Those who are the great remnant of God's people. Those who are born again and make up His Body. Those believers coming together for fellowship, edification, comfort, and training.

The local church or fellowship is that place where

God's warriors rally together for advancement and promotion which becomes a refreshing refuge for suffering humanity. It's a place where all are loved, forgiven, and accepted and where the Lord is exalted as King through worship and praise. The local church is not a building, a name, a piece of equipment, or money, even though it would be hard to organize and mobilize without all of this. What is the church? You and me, friend—members in particular!

CHAPTER 2
THE OPPOSITION

THE DEVIL

We all find that religion, and the people who are indoctrinated in it, will be one of your greatest obstacles. It's easy to see that even Jesus was faced with this opposition to the truth much of the time. In fact, the Gospel account of Matthew, chapter 15, verses 2-9, explains to us the deadly effects of tradition. Jesus was being challenged by religious rulers as to why His disciples didn't follow the tradition of the elders. The issue was the washing of hands before meals. Jesus' reply was quite simple. He told them in verse 4, ". . . For God commanded . . ." and in verse 5, ". . . But ye say . . ."

We can see today that this is still a major problem. The religious, traditional crowd is always doing and saying that which is contrary to what God says. How does this become an opposition to the truth? Two ways. The first Jesus explained well in verse 6 of this same passage:

"Thus have ye made the commandment of God of none effect by your tradition."

Tradition will nullify God's Word in those who follow after it. Secondly, most people are carnally-minded. We have been brought up hearing and studying man's problems of life and how to solve them. When religious leaders rise up against you and spread false rumors and such, it's easy for people to want to go along. Can they win over you? Certainly not!

It was the religious crowd that followed Jesus around trying to trap Him in His sayings. They told Him He had a devil and finally paid someone to betray Him. It was the religious rulers who brought Him to Pilate and took Him to the cross. Watch out for the leaven of Pharisees (Matt. 16:6-12). It's one of your most dangerous oppositions.

PERSECUTION

"Yea, and all that will live godly in Christ Jesus shall suffer persecution."

2 Timothy 3:12

You and I both know that persecution is not enjoyable, and neither of us is probably going to pray for more. Nevertheless, this scripture is true. If you're a pastor, begin to do things godly, rule that local church with authority, and teach people their rights and privileges in Christ, and you'll see that the persecution will rise up against you. So what!

"For what if some did not believe? shall their unbelief make the faith of God without effect?

God forbid: yea, let God be true, but every man a liar; as it is written, That thou mightest be justified in thy sayings, and mightest overcome when thou art judged."

Romans 3:3-4

"Blessed are ye, when men shall revile you, and persecute you, and shall say all manner of evil against you falsely, for my sake.

Rejoice, and be exceeding glad: for great is your reward in heaven: for so persecuted they the prophets which were before you."

Matthew 5:11-12

So what if they are spreading rumors. So what if they are saying things that are not true. So what if they are trying to discredit your name and the work you are doing for Christ. If you are building a house for God and He is working with you confirming the Word, you will look fruitful in due season, and they will look terribly barren.

TIME

Time seems to be a terrible opposition for young ministers and churches in embryo stages. There are no shortcuts with God. Promotion and advancement come only from Him (Ps. 75:6-7). Don't be ashamed of the stage you are in but rather notice the rustling of the leaves in the trees and know the move is on (2 Sam. 5:23-24). Humble yourself in the sight of the Lord, and He will lift you up (James 4:10).

For everything there is a season and a perfect timing of the Lord. Sure, there is a lot to do. Yes, there is a lot of equipment you need to buy. Many local churches are still believing God for a building to put the flock in. Read Ecclesiastes 3:1-8. It will help to remind you that God is at work on your behalf. In due season He will lift you up.

MONEY

Here is a subject on which all of us need a daily reminder. Money is not our god, nor is it our source of supply. Oh sure, it's nice to have a bunch of it. It's good to receive great offerings. Pastors need money in order to do all that God has given them to do. But don't live from offering to offering. Don't say that you can't do things because you don't have enough money.

Listen to this small testimony. I was pastoring a baby church, and we were meeting in a rented hall. It was a horrible place to have church. We would have to go in to clean up the room before each service because it had been rented out for dances, rock concerts, wedding receptions, and similar things. We had to sweep up cigarette butts, mop up beer from the floor, and cover the beer tap with something so our children wouldn't see it.

I remember a rustproofing business next door. This building was attached to ours and after a full day of undercoating cars, that smell had seeped into our rented room. When the weather was hot and sticky, those fumes would make our eyes water and even made some people nauseated. I tell you, that place looked as rough as it smelled. But we were rejoicing that we even had a place that would rent to us so we could have meetings. We had already outgrown our home basement, and so onward we went!

I didn't realize it at first, but that meeting place began to form certain ideas in me. I began to say things like, "When we get our own building, we will buy that piece of machinery," or "When we get more people, we will be able to do that," or "When the church is a couple of years old, the offerings will be better and . . ." I said things like this so often I even had our congregation thinking and speaking this way. The Lord showed me one day that we would never get our own building or have a larger attendance or receive larger offerings if we didn't mature what we had already.

You see, I was living in the future portion of our

vision rather than the present. When I realized this, we began to fix up our meeting place and do the best with what we had. Some people would say, "Don't put any money into that project; it'll just be wasted when we move." We didn't listen to this but rather dug in. We began to confess and believe for money NOW, wisdom NOW, and completion of projects NOW. Do you know what we found out? Money was never a stable obstacle of ours. Each time it yelled out to us in lack or poverty, we would not submit to it or confess it. Even now that the church has grown so well and so fast, we still dethrone mammon when it tries to take the place of Jesus.

There are many obstacles and oppositions that are trying to stop you. By no means are they all listed in this little book. Some of them will seem to be unique to your situation. Remember though, no temptation will come upon you that is not common to man, and with each Jesus makes a way of escape (1 Cor. 10:13).

Stand with God, and see His hand of salvation.

CHAPTER 3
FIRST THINGS FIRST

THE CALLING

My friends, it isn't enough to desire the office of pastor or even see the need for a local work in your area. In order for that work to be in the perfect will of God and be productive, you must be called of God to start it and nourished by God to perfect it. He will give sufficiency and growth. He will give you wisdom and success. When Jesus, the Head of the Church, places you in that office, directs you to a certain city, and gives you instructions on what He wants done, then all there is to do is be obedient to Him, and He will finish the work. Save yourself and others a shipwreck by assuring that you are called by God and that He has given you the vision before you attempt to bring it to pass.

PRAYER AND FASTING

As I mentioned in the previous chapter, there are many obstacles and opposing forces with which you will have to contend. This is going to have to be done through prayer. It's good to have intercessions, but that is no substitute for your personal prayer time. Isaiah, chapter 58, tells us why we are to fast properly:

- To loose the bands of wickedness.

- To undo the heavy burdens.

- To let the oppressed go free.

- To break every yoke.

- To deal thy bread to the hungry.

- Thy light shall break forth as the morning.

- Thy health shall spring forth speedily.

- Thy righteousness shall go before thee.

- The Lord will answer your call.

- The Lord will guide thee.

I remember the eight months before we started the Midland church. We fasted and prayed together with our staff and intercessors every Monday night. What a difference it made. When we moved to the city God gave us and began to fulfill the vision He gave us, it seemed like all we had to do was reap. Much of the warfare had already been done.

THE VISION

Know where you are going, what you are going to accomplish when you get there, and how you plan to do it. You and I both know that we walk by faith. God is not going to show you every little detail in the beginning. He will reveal it to you one step at a time. However, He most likely will show you much of the skeleton outline, or major points, to the work He wants you to do.

Learn to write things down. A simple illustration is how some people will remember so well the exact date they were born again but will so easily forget why they were or even how they were. Write down the vision. Put it on paper. Why? So those who read it may run with it. Even if it is for an appointed time, it will surely come to pass. By writing it down, you will stay on course and know what to follow next.

PATIENCE

Don't be in such a hurry. God isn't! Relax and serve Him well. Serve Him and not the vision or the church. Worship and praise Him. Talk about Him. Wait on Him and His perfect season. You will see that you will reap in due season if you faint not (Gal. 6:9).

CHAPTER 4
ORGANIZATION

A lot of good brethren today shy away from organization. It seems to be "whatever the Spirit leads." I know we need to be led by the Spirit, but that doesn't mean to walk in the dark—it's a walk in the light. Many pastors who have come out of denominational backgrounds were so organized and had to follow a format so rigorously that now they are almost paranoid about formats. I know we shouldn't get so organized that the Holy Spirit is blocked from our meetings, but I also know that organization will eliminate confusion and display quality in all we do. Remember, the Lord wants us to have all things done decently, in order, and for the edification of the church.

DECLARATION

Once again, I would like to express the importance of writing and declaring the vision. Put it on paper and fliers, in the news, and teach it to those fellowshipping with you. Make known to others your form of governments and the way they can be of help to you.

In order to organize, you must meet with people and over and over again describe to them the vision and their part. One at a time they will catch on and hook up to what God is doing.

FOUNDATION

A good pastor who is wise will lay a supreme foundation before he even tries to build the house of the Lord. Take lots of time to do this. The better the foundation, the stronger the building. What do I mean by foundation? Draw the people together in unity so you are all talking, thinking, and doing the same thing. You may choose to teach a series of classes on basic doctrine. You may choose to expound on the vision or the particular details of the future work. Regardless of what areas you describe, all of you must walk in agreement and unity together.

Here's a little hint: be specific, honest, and simple. People admire those who say profound things but usually don't learn much from them and have a hard time following them.

WORSHIP AND WORD

These are a must to have as part of your fellowship. They must show up in the lives of the individual believer as well as in corporate meetings. The Bible says in Zechariah 14:16-18, "No worship, no rain." If any local church or fellowship is going to be productive for the Lord, it is going to have to have signs, wonders, miracles, gifts, baptisms, and people saved. "No worship, no rain." How will you have any one of these things? By having the presence of the Lord. Worship Him and praise Him. Teach the people to participate and also allow plenty of time for it in your services. Magnify His name and exalt His throne. Let the world know that you are not afraid or ashamed to demonstrate your love and worship for the Lord. Shout, sing, clap, lift your hands, dance, and bow to the King of Kings. Will some be offended at all of this? Sure. But not the ones who love His Word (Ps. 119:165). Will it offend the Lord? Certainly not. He'll dwell in your presence. The more you worship and praise Him, the more you'll witness His presence and the more spiritual blessing (rain) you'll receive.

What about the Word? Give it first place and teach it without compromise. Live what you teach, and you'll see others living it also. The Bible must be your highest standard of authority and rulership. Teach people to go to it for help and direction. When people see that everything you do lines up with the Bible, they will line up with you. Besides, it is God's Word that is confirmed when He works with us. Speak it boldly, just as the apostles, by stretching forth your hand to heal so that signs and wonders will be done in the name of the holy child, Jesus (Acts 4:29-30).

CHAPTER 5
GOVERNMENTS

How important are church governments? Very important. One can have the quality in any given thing, but if it isn't governed properly, most of it will go to waste. As I read the Bible, I see more and more clearly how God used leaders. When He didn't have one, He raised one up. When He had one who wasn't doing right, He raised up a replacement. I also can see in the Bible how much people need leaders. When they didn't have one, they began to worship idols and sin against God. When they had a bad one, they followed and were wiped out by the enemy. When they had a good leader, they produced greatly and glorified God.

WHAT DO WE MEAN—GOVERNMENTS?

Governments - the leaders of the local church and their system of ruling, guarding, equipping, and mobilizing the saints.

Study the following local church government outline and see how smoothly and accurately things can be done. If everyone performs their ministry with all of their heart, mind, and strength, nothing will be left undone, and everyone will be plenty busy.

GOVERNMENT HEAD

DEITY
- Jehovah – Supreme Ruler and Father
- Jesus – Head of the Church
- Holy Spirit – Divine Director

HUMANITY
- Pastor; overseer; responsible shepherd

MINISTRY OF HELPS

MINISTERIAL STAFF
- Associate minister
- Helps minister
- Worship minister
- Teen minister
- Children's minister
- Infant's minister

ELDERSHIP MINISTRY
- Spiritual matters of the people
- Visitation

DEACONSHIP MINISTRY
- Material matters
- Business
- Maintenance

BOARD OF TRUSTEES

CORPORATE AND LEGAL AID

You and I both know that no one man is more respected by the Lord than another. Each of us are equal, and we should be blessed equally in our relationship to the Father. Even so, all through the Bible we can see how God anointed certain men to be leaders, and He gave those leaders authority. Authority was given to those leaders because God made them responsible for the people. When people are responsible, then they must give an account for that area of responsibility. If they must give an account, then they need to have governing ability (authority) in order to perform in that God-given responsibility and produce results. So it isn't that some are better or more favored than others but rather that some are held more accountable than others.

In any organization there must be one person to govern. Someone has to be responsible. Someone has to say yes or no. Some people say it is dangerous for one man (a pastor) to rule the church and make decisions. They feel that it would be safer to have a board of voters. They actually think that five people can hear from the Lord better than one. History proves that God has had trouble getting mankind to listen and obey. Having one head instead of five reduces the odds of "mishearing" by 80 percent. How's that? Well, most board members know very little about pastoring and, in fact, very little about God. They are not used to hearing; they are dull of hearing. Each person, including the pastor, has a chance of not hearing or misunderstanding what God said. Narrow down the rate of misunderstanding, and go "pastoral rule." One more thing, let Jesus choose the pastor. It works much better that way!

If each ministry is doing their job supernaturally, the pastor will be able to hear accurately because he will spend his time doing it. He won't have to be visiting if the elders are. He won't have to be working with his hands if the deacons are. He won't be setting up and warming up the church if the ministry of helps is doing their jobs.

THE MINISTERIAL STAFF

This is the staff of ordained or licensed ministers

whom the pastor has chosen (with direction from the Lord) to be his pulpit and advisory aides. He will explain to them the areas of responsibility each will have. These vary with each pastor and also according to the needs of the church. Basically, they will take care of the teaching and administration of the church and carry out the Lord's vision as the senior pastor prescribes.

THE ELDERSHIP MINISTRY (Exodus 18:13-23)

This is the staff of qualified elders in the church (1 Tim. 3:1-7) who will take on the spiritual oversight. They should be visiting the flock, giving counsel and wisdom. They should be reporting severe matters to the pastor. These are the men who have authority to visit the hospitals, jails, homes, etc. They are not a voting board of church rulers. They are spiritual watchmen of the flock. Remember, watch the flock, not the pastorate!

THE DEACONSHIP MINISTRY

This is the staff of people who will be waiting on tables, thus relieving the pastors so they will have time for the Word and prayer. Once again, they do not run the church or make governmental decisions. In many local churches they will be used as, and perhaps even titled, "ushers."

THE BOARD OF TRUSTEES

This is the staff of people who will be aides to the pastor in corporate affairs and legal advice. They will not be the rulers of the church from a pastorate position. They may or may not be part of the local work. Some may even live in another city. They will deal with the local governments, state governments, federal government, Internal

Revenue Service, and other legal corporate matters.

WHY GOVERNMENTS?

Jesus has a job to get done—harvesting the souls of humanity. Whom will He use? His Body—the Church. The only way this will ever happen is for us believers (the Church) to submit to the men of authority Christ has set in the Church.

Many times when you say "submit," people misunderstand. No man has the right to lord over and rule over you as a dictator. Submission is nothing more than protection for the submitter. It is saying that you recognize a higher authority and you unite yourself with that authority. You see, each one of us has a certain authority. When we submit, we simply let another person of higher authority know that we unify our authority with theirs. Is it godly? Yes. Read Romans 13:1-8.

MORE FACTS ON THIS SUBJECT
- Ephesians 4:11-13
- Jeremiah 3:15, 23:3-4
- 1 Peter 5:1-5
- 1 Thessalonians 5:12-13

WHY GOVERNMENTS IF JESUS IS THE HEAD?
- To teach church discipline
- To keep all things edifying
- To keep all things in divine order
- To inform all people of the vision
- To stop the confusing attack of the evil one
- To define the Lord's direction (His messengers)

CHAPTER 6
LEGAL AND RIGHT

We need to do all that we can to give the Church a good reputation. The Bible tells us that a good name is to be chosen above riches (Prov. 22:1). Too many businessmen have a poor outlook on the Church. It should be that the public and the government would choose to do business with us over anyone else because of our loyalty and quality.

Pastoring a local church is, in many ways, corporate business. Much needs to be done in the form of paperwork, communications, public relations, advertising, legal matters, and accounting. I suggest that as you need professional aid, find some. Keep yourself clean and honest.

PUBLIC RELATIONS

Every state, county, and city has rules that pertain to ministers and churches. It is very wise for a pastor to visit the local law library to do his homework. Look up the laws pertaining to areas you are involved in, such as solemnizing weddings, funerals, baptisms, dedications, jail and hospital visitations, etc. Know your rights.

I also recommend that you contact local civic authorities and inform them of your meeting times, locations, and purposes. Visit such people as the mayor, sheriff, chief of police, etc. Notify the city police, chamber of commerce, and newspaper of your whereabouts and purpose. All of this will spell quality and excellence to those being notified.

MINISTERIAL RECORDS

Keep a copy of each legal letter, news release, advertisement, and publication that involves you or the church. This will help if you ever need to refer to, or are questioned about, specific meetings.

Keep a good, up-to-date church calendar which includes your ministerial activities. You should keep these calendars on file for future reference. They will help you, as they will show all of your appointments (place, time, date) for the past year.

Keep a record of all people who have been baptized, married, or buried under your ministry, and also baby dedications. Write down names, mailing addresses, dates, etc.

Keep a typed copy of each speech, public address, or sermon you've done. Date them and put them in notebooks by year. This will be a big aid to you if you ever wish to use the material again. Who knows, perhaps you'll become famous, and someone will want to make a book out of all your sermon outlines!

LEGAL FILES

I will write about keeping records of financial matters in the chapter called "Finances," but other files are just as important. You, as the pastor, should keep the church in proper legal status. You should be in contact with the government in corporate matters. Seek legal advice to help you in these areas. Always duplicate and date all correspondence to the government. This will aid you in the case of them misplacing something or it being lost in the mail. Also keep records of all phone calls with the government including times, persons talked to, dates, and results of conversation.

All seals, certificates, and letters from the government offices should be kept in good files. A pastor (even though he may have good legal advisors) should keep himself up-to-date on IRS, federal, and state legal terms and codes.

Be a wise leader—lead with wisdom!

Note: Please don't assume that others are doing all of this for you the way you like it. Teach your helpers and then check on them. Keep a constant means of communication with them. You are responsible, pastor.

CHAPTER 7
THE MINISTRY OF HELPS

The harvest is huge. The vision is huge. The workload is huge. How will any one man do it? He won't! Every pastor needs helpers. God knows this, so He has defined this ministry in the Bible for our instruction and benefit.

Why don't a lot of pastors have enough help? They haven't properly trained people. Many pastors are wanting to "believe in" their helpers. They are wishing and hoping that they will come from somewhere else, already trained and ready to go to work. Well, some might come that way, but most will not. The Bible very simply teaches us pastors that it is our job to train the people of the Lord to do the work of the ministry (Eph. 4:11-12).

For years we have quoted the scripture from Matthew and said, "The harvest truly is plenteous, but the laborers are few." I have good news for you, pastors. Praise God, the laborers are no longer few. There are many, many potential workers in the Church today. When Jesus spoke this to His disciples, the laborers truly were few. Jesus at one time had many disciples, but just like people today, they became discouraged or perhaps they misunderstood. What happened to them? The Bible says that they went back and walked with Him no more (John 6:66-70). They quit! They simply quit being disciples and went back to their own way of living. How sad. That left only twelve disciples—and Jesus said one out of the twelve was a devil. No matter how you look at it, that is few laborers. But you see, that was years ago. The Church has grown from eleven true disciples to hundreds of thousands of them. No, folks, the laborers are no longer few. They are many. We need to pray that the Lord will send them forth. How can He? When we pastors have trained them.

Let me show you in Acts, chapter 6, what happens when the ministry of helps has been put into operation by the leadership:

> *"And in those days, when the number of the disciples was multiplied, there arose a murmuring of the Grecians against the Hebrews, because their widows were neglected in the daily ministration.*
>
> *Then the twelve called the multitude of the disciples unto them, and said, It is not reason that we should leave the word of God, and serve tables.*
>
> *Wherefore, brethren, look ye out among you seven men of honest report, full of the Holy Ghost and wisdom, whom we may appoint over this business.*
>
> *But we will give ourselves continually to prayer, and to the ministry of the word.*
>
> *And the saying pleased the whole multitude: and they chose Stephen, a man full of faith and of the Holy Ghost, and Philip, and Prochorus, and Nicanor, and Timon, and Parmenas, and Nicolas a proselyte of Antioch:*
>
> *Whom they set before the apostles: and when they had prayed, they laid their hands on them.*

And the word of God increased; and the number of the disciples multiplied in Jerusalem greatly; and a great company of the priests were obedient to the faith.

And Stephen, full of faith and power, did great wonders and miracles among the people."

Acts 6:1-8

If you'll notice, it was written in verse 1 that certain things were being neglected in the daily ministration of the church.

Verse 2: The apostles taught the disciples that it was not good or profitable for them to leave the Word of God to work with their hands.

Verses 5 and 6: Men full of faith and the Holy Ghost were chosen to do the daily work.

Verse 7: Here are the results: 1) the Word of God increased, 2) the number of disciples multiplied greatly, and 3) a company of the priests were obedient to the faith.

Oh, how we need helpers! Oh, how we need the Father to send them forth—not send them away—send them forth! Many think to go forth in ministry is to leave the local church. I have listed the following information that should help your church better organize or mobilize the ministry of helps. Please feel free to use what you can.

Note: I would like to refer you to chapter 5 on Governments to refresh you regarding the ministerial staff, elder staff, deacon staff, and board of trustees.

JOB DESCRIPTIONS

PASTOR AND WIFE
- Study Word of God

- Live a disciplined life
- Pray
- Organize
- Guard
- Live holy
- Feed
- Train believers to do the work
- Have direct oversight of everything and everybody

ASSOCIATE PASTORS

- Direct aide to pastor and wife
- Authoritative head in absence of pastor and wife
- Representative of pastor in other churches
- Aid in oversight and advisor to all
- Personal counselor of church
- Missions coordinator
- Guest ministries scheduler
- Intercessor for all ministries and staff personnel

MINISTER OF EDUCATION

- Oversight of Bible Training Center
- Oversight of Audio Department
- Oversight of Video Department
- Oversight of Publications Department
- Coordinate education programs
- Teach other teachers
- Pray for increase of God's Word and its free course
- Pray for all who teach in the church

MINISTER OF WORSHIP

- Lead and oversee all worship in church and other meetings

- Teach worship
- Train other worship leaders
- Be responsible for all overhead transparencies and machinery
- Oversee all special music and singers in church
- Oversee orchestra
- Program all music specials
- Gather all musicians before service (be sure they are ready)
- Pray for all involved in worship and music ministry

YOUTH PASTOR/DIRECTOR OF TEENS

- Hold regular teen meetings
- Counsel teens in matters pertaining to their age
- Hold regular teen activities for fun and fellowship
- Pray for all teens

CHILDREN'S MINISTER

- Hold regular children's meetings during all adult meetings
- Be responsible for spiritual growth of children
- Counsel with parents on children's lifestyle (spiritual)
- Provide materials for parents and children at home (devotionals)
- Be available to hold meetings outside of church
- Train other children's ministers and helpers
- Pray for all the children in church

DIRECTOR OF INFANT MINISTRIES

- Organize and supervise all nursery meetings
- Choose and train all nursery workers

- Be responsible for upkeep and cleaning nursery facilities
- Be responsible to provide all nursery materials
- Pray for all children in each nursery meeting
- Greet all parents and keep them well informed

PASTOR'S INTERCESSOR

- Pray constantly for pastor, wife, and children
- Be available to attend all intercessor meetings
- Be ready to train other personal intercessors
- Report all revelation received during prayer to pastor
- Confess and pray good things over pastor and family

DIRECTOR OF INTERCESSION

- Hold regular intercession meetings
- Do spiritual warfare for church and ministry
- Confess prosperity in all areas
- Oversee telephone prayer ministry
- Keep pastor informed

RESIDING EVANGELIST

- Go, in the name of Jesus, as a representative of the church
- Train other evangelists
- Advise pastor on outreach and input in other churches visited
- Keep wife and children in meetings while you are away
- Pray for population increase in local church through salvation

HEAD ELDER

- Have direct oversight of all people
- Aid pastor in spiritual church activities
- Be able to teach from time to time as pastor requests
- Oversee staff of elders
- Obtain monthly reports from each elder and present to pastor
- Hold periodic elder meetings for purpose of prayer and fellowship
- Oversee all visitation of elders
- Pray for all elders

ELDERS ON STAFF

- Supervise sheep during public gatherings
- Guard sheep on a daily basis
- Be a spiritual aide to all members of church
- Take care of widows and fatherless (spiritual needs)
- Visit fatherless, widows, sick, poor, needy
- Oversee outreach to nursing homes, jails, hospitals, new converts
- Serve on church communion board
- Be available to serve on church ushering staff and altar crew
- Pray for spiritual prosperity and well being of all members

HEAD DEACON OR HEAD USHER

- Have direct oversight of deacon staff
- Have direct oversight of security and safety in all meetings
- Have direct oversight of usher and altar teams

- Have direct oversight of executive deacons
- Have direct oversight of all working crews
- Have direct oversight of church janitorial crews
- Have direct oversight of hostess teams
- Have direct oversight of buildings, lights, snow removal, etc.
- Obtain deacons' monthly reports and present to pastor
- Pray for all deacons on staff
- Be responsible to believe in all finances

DEACONS OR USHERS ON STAFF

- Be available to help on any projects for widows
- Be available to work on any work crews
- Be available to work on any janitorial crews
- Be available to be used for ushering and altar crews
- Pray for all those who are involved in helping on work projects
- Pray for other deacons

EXECUTIVE DEACON OR EXECUTIVE USHER

- Watch for any special visiting ministers
- Be personal aide to pastor before and after each meeting
- Be responsible to transport ministers to and from airport, hotel, etc.
- Escort ladies to and from platform during meetings
- Run special errands for pastor
- Be responsible for security of platform and all special guests
- Be equipped to be pastor's driver

- Assure that speakers have microphones, water, etc.

TEACHER

- Teach the Word and not personal views or convictions
- Support pastor's staff with all presentations
- Pray over all lessons and those who will hear

HEAD COUNSELOR

- Be ready at all altar services to aid those who respond
- Be responsible for preservice prayer meetings
- Pray for all to come to repentance (new converts)
- Pray for response to Word of the Lord
- Have materials ready for those who respond to altar call
- Train other altar counselors

DIRECTOR OF SINGLES

- Hold regular meetings for singles to teach and fellowship
- Provide regular prayer meetings
- Refer counseling to elders in charge
- Pray for all singles

HOST/HOSTESS

- Arrive early for each service
- Pray and be ready to minister
- Be an example in dress, speech, and attitude
- Greet each person who comes and pass out information needed
- Inform newcomers of available children and infant ministries

- Pray for all to feel loved and welcomed

AUDIO TECHNICIAN

- Make sure all machinery is ready for the meeting
- Set up, take down, transport, operate, and maintain all equipment
- Train other audio technicians (have at least one good substitute)
- Pray over equipment—improvements, additions, operation

AUDIOCASSETTE MINISTRY

- Oversee operation, care, and security of all equipment
- Train others (have at least one good substitute)
- Duplicate all ordered cassettes
- Present all duplicated cassettes to bookstore sales-persons
- Maintain catalog of all masters
- Be responsible for all masters
- Oversee Tape-of-the-Month Club
- Pray that all recorded messages help the hearers

SALESPERSON

- Set up tape and book sales
- Set up and sell all guest ministries' books and tapes
- Gather all monies for books and tapes and present to Financial Department
- Distribute all ordered books and tapes
- Pray for increase of sales

PUBLIC RELATIONS PERSON

- Oversee all advertising

- Coordinate all seminars, conventions, etc.
- Correspond with other churches, ministries, etc.
- Develop relations with businesses
- Coordinate all ministerial travel with agents

I should note here that I have given you a skeleton of the ministry of helps. This was to give you ideas that will help you organize your local work. There is much that can be added to this skeleton either by adding other ministry jobs or enlarging the responsibilities of the ones I gave.

I would also like to note here that though organization is good and gives people a form to work from, it will still produce little without the anointing that breaks every yoke. The key, pastors, is to show people that these ministry of helps areas are supernatural jobs, and it takes anointed people to handle them. God knows how many people you are equipped to handle properly. As you prepare for more (by increasing the supernatural helps ministry), He'll send you more.

A reminder—don't keep saying you'll do this and that when the church grows larger or when you have more people or more money. Train the people now to do each ministry. Be ready. God could send an extra hundred people to your next midweek service.

IF THE WORK IS NOT GETTING DONE

If the work is not getting done, don't blame the people. If the attendance is poor, don't blame the people. If the offerings are low, don't blame the people. They are what you've taught them. They will perform the way you train them. They will follow the way you lead them.

It is your job, pastor, to train them to do the work and oversee it so it's done right!

CHAPTER 8
GOD'S WONDERFUL PEOPLE

Dealing every day with people can be both a pleasure and a heartbreak. The pastor's daily schedule will involve meetings with all kinds of people—from those truly serving God to those who refuse to admit there is a God. Even in the local church there is quite a variety of people. It is up to the pastor to seek out those who are faithful.

> *"And the things that thou hast heard of me among many witnesses, the same commit thou to faithful men, who shall be able to teach others also."*
>
> 2 Timothy 2:2

I have learned as a pastor that faithfulness in a person is the supreme quality. Many people are talented, prosperous, and eager to be used. It really doesn't matter how well they can do if they don't show up to do it. Take a hint, my friend, watch for those who prove to be faithful.

Don't be afraid of people who seem to have a track record of failure. Most of the home run kings of baseball strike out many times before they set the records. You will find that the time you spend training people who are not already successful will be some of the best time you can invest. People appreciate leaders who help make them a success and train them to do well.

On the contrary, investing time in people who are already talented or feel they are already talented or feel they are already trained will put you in a position of sometimes bumping noses. Why? Because these people normally aren't as grateful as those who really want to help. These same people seem to always have a better idea than you and constantly want to make a suggestion. It is a privilege to train all of God's people, but it is a double blessing to take a person who is not victorious and make them that way. Look at the following scriptures:

> *"David therefore departed thence, and escaped to the cave Adullam: and when his brethren and all his father's house heard it, they went down thither to him.*
>
> *And every one that was in distress, and every one that was in debt, and every one that was discontented, gathered themselves unto him; and he became a captain over them: and there were with him about four hundred men."*
>
> 1 Samuel 22:1-2
>
> *"These be the names of the mighty men whom David had . . ."*
>
> 2 Samuel 23:8

What a challenge! How exciting! In these scriptures we read how men who were distressed, in debt, and discontent ran into a cave after a man of God. Then we read that this certain man of God became a captain over the other 400. Praise God!

Now in 2 Samuel 23:8, we see that this David had mighty men who performed mighty tasks for the kingdom.

What happened in that cave? Seek it out, pastor, and cause your local church to be that cave—a spiritual factory of godly men.

ROOM TO GROW

Allow people the beautiful pleasure of growing under your ministry. People need discipline, and they expect you to be fair and honest about it. People need you to tell them the truth. They want to be trained and well equipped for the ministry.

I have found that the majority of God's people truly want to stop playing and start working. They have a real hunger to be established in the ministry God has for them. It is the pastor's job to do this. He is to train them to do the work of the ministry.

GIVE THEM PASTORAL ATTENTION

Use the Bible for great wisdom to discipline and counsel God's flock. Remember that they are anointed, and we are to touch not His anointed. In the same way, they are to do His prophets no harm. Don't abuse or misuse the people of the Lord. At the same time, don't be afraid to discipline them or correct them.

Learn to let people be themselves. You do not want to produce a whole line of identical people. It is the pastor's job to build character in the hearts and minds of people. What makes the church beautiful is that God created everyone just a tiny bit different so we could be individuals. Let people be who they are. Just change what they are. You'll see that this will be much easier, and your church will be much more successful for the Lord.

People love attention. I believe they have a right to be in touch with the local shepherd. I don't think they need to rob all of his time through counseling, phone calls, or altar attacks. Great encouragement comes from a pat on the back or a smile from their pastor. Sometimes a look of pleasure or satisfaction on pastor's face in response to their project or accomplishment is all that is needed.

Be sensitive to the flock of God. Stay in touch with them and love them, but remember—you are the shepherd Jesus has placed over His people.

CHAPTER 9
FINANCES

There is so much to be said about finances. In order to cover it properly, you should seek out books and tapes that do nothing but teach on this subject.

I am going to touch on just a couple of different issues that pertain directly to the pioneer pastor and the new local church.

BOOK WORK

It is a must to have very good book work right from the beginning. Records should be kept of all income and expenditures as well as a current mailing list of all donors. All accounts, loans, and checkbooks should be kept up-to-date and be balanced properly. Start right from the beginning to be a good, accurate steward of God's money. I very highly recommend that you seek out some mature, professional advice on this subject as soon as possible. The longer you do without it, the more you'll have to make up.

TITHES/SOWING SEED

A word to the wise is—give your tithe. Each pastor has to come to the revelation of this. At our local church, we tithe of our total income. We tithe it to another church which has helped or blessed us. Why? Not because we have to, but because we know it's right, it works, and it's biblical. Giving to the poor is also very important. Try to figure out a good benevolence system. You'll have to seek the Lord for special wisdom. Try not to hand out money to just anyone who comes by, yet don't be afraid to give to strangers. Also, use some caution and discretion when you are going to help people within the church. It's sad to say, some will try to take unfair advantage of the system. It will take godly wisdom to be able to give liberally yet justly to all who are in need.

Even though it is good to help those in need, teach the people that they are to give and support the gospel ministry, not vice versa.

Giving to other ministries is a must. Start right from the beginning to give generously to honest missionaries and to other local churches. Many churches today hold up this kind of giving until they get larger and have larger offerings. Guess what. Having more people doesn't always mean larger offerings, but more sowing into other ministries is a guaranteed cause of prosperity in your church.

BELIEVING GOD

Use all the scripture, faith, and confession you can to bring in the material things you need. God wants you to have a nice facility, good equipment, and all your bills paid.

Turn to the people and teach them about tithing and giving. The Bible says that the people are to bring every natural substance to the priests in order for the house of the Lord to be built (Ex. 25:1-9).

A word of caution here—as you turn to the people for help (and the receiving of offerings), don't turn to them as your source. You only turn to the people so they can have a part and also be obedient to the vision.

Every new work has some struggles with paying a pastor's salary. Use your faith. You, pastors, are the best asset the church has. You be sure to draw at least a small portion as seed faith toward a good income. If you have to work for a while on a secular job until the church grows, then do what you must. Be careful about looking to your secular profession as a source. The devil would like to work you to death being both full-time in a job and in the ministry.

The keys to financial prosperity in the local church are:

- Teach and confess the uncompromised Word of God.

- Tithe and give liberally and with wisdom.

- Put works to your faith.

- Turn to God as your source of supply.

- Teach the people to tithe and give scripturally.

Remember to stay clean, be honest, and believe God. You will have a very prosperous work.

CHAPTER 10
DON'T QUIT

". . . Write the vision, and make it plain upon tables, that he may run that readeth it.

For the vision is yet for an appointed time, but at the end it shall speak, and not lie: though it tarry, wait for it; because it will surely come, it will not tarry.

Behold, his soul which is lifted up is not upright in him: but the just shall live by his faith."

Habakkuk 2:2-4

Do God, yourself, and the Body of Christ a great favor—don't quit! Stick it out! Stand in there! Refuse to lose!

The devil knows that you have been equipped and anointed to do what God has called you to. He knows that God is the One who has put that vision in your heart. He also knows that he cannot beat you, destroy you, or overcome the Word of the Lord in you.

The devil's number one objective is to get you to quit. If he can just get you to quit and lay down your weapons and your armor, he has won. If he can just get you into discouragement and cause you to lay down the vision, he has won. As long as you fight, you win. As long as you press toward the mark of the prize of the high calling of God—you win. As long as you refuse to lay down and quit—you win. By examining Habakkuk 2:2-4, we can easily see the format we are to follow as believers.

Many people think the vision is passing by them and all they have to do is reach out and grab hold of it. Not so! God has declared the vision. Every vision has a beginning and an end. It begins when God transfers it from His throne room into your heart. Each portion of the vision has been appointed a perfect time to unfold before your eyes. But it isn't passing by you as you stand still and wait for it. You must walk through it. As long as you are progressing forward for the Lord, you will continue to see new ramifications and stages of the vision. As long as you walk hand in hand with the Master, He will walk you through the vision, keeping you in His perfect will and timing. For everything there is a season.

Once again, drawing your attention to Habakkuk 2:2-4, you'll see the proper manner in which we should walk with the vision (a step at a time) that the Lord has given us.

> "... *Write the vision, and make it plain* ..."
>
> Habakkuk 2:2

1. Most believers have not yet learned to write down what God has shown them. Don't rely on your memory. Please write things down.

2. Many believers, especially leaders in the Kingdom, lose track of the main points of the vision. They end up being sidetracked by a minute detail of the vision. This causes them to get out of the timing of the Lord. Proper

Word and prayer time will help to keep your mind and heart fixed on the overall vision.

". . . Make it plain upon tables . . ."

Habakkuk 2:2

If you will write down the main steps to the vision God has given you, you will see that those main parts will be stepping stones to the end (fulfillment) of your vision. Making it simple and bold before your eyes and the eyes of followers will only enhance their appetite to hook up.

"For the vision is yet for an appointed time . . ."

Habakkuk 2:3

Simply said, this means it's not going to "poof" into existence! It's not a cram course or the waving of a magic wand. No matter what stage of the vision you are walking in, you will see that some of it has already come to pass. You will also see that some of it is being manifested this very moment, but some is yet to be revealed or manifested at a later date. It doesn't matter if it all isn't happening now because "at the end it shall speak."

If the vision is truly from the Lord, then as you walk through it and it is manifested in its time stages, all beholders will see that it is of the Lord. The fruit and results of the vision are proof enough.

". . . Though it tarry, wait for it . . ."

Habakkuk 2:3

Don't quit. Even if it seems like nothing is happening and no one is hooking up with you, don't quit. Portions of the vision will tarry. So what! That doesn't mean it isn't coming to pass. Keep walking with the Master. Every step you take activates progression. Wait for it! Keep busy. Before you even realize it, you will walk into another section of God's best for you.

Let me share with you a quick illustration. A man is sitting at the airport waiting to board his plane. He has a two-hour layover. If that man sits watching the clock, asking the airline personnel continuously if everything is okay, and pacing back and forth, those two hours are going to seem like two days. Why? Because he is not busy. He is waiting impatiently. He has his eyes on one thing—the fulfillment of his goal: getting on that plane.

But the same man in the same situation can attain his goal with much greater pleasure. How? Simply by staying busy doing things until it's time. Before he knows it, they will be announcing the boarding of his plane—probably to his surprise.

It's the same in the Kingdom of God. Don't wait passively until the next portion comes your way. It will seem like a long time. Do what you can. Stay busy with the portion at hand. The vision will surely come!

> *"And let us not be weary in well doing: for in due season we shall reap, if we faint not."*
>
> Galatians 6:9

Do God, yourself, and the Body of Christ a great favor—don't quit!

PRAYER OF SALVATION

YOU CAN BE SAVED FROM ETERNAL DAMNA-TION and get God's help now in this life. All you have to do is humble your heart, believe in Christ's work at Calvary for you, and pray the prayer below.

Dear Heavenly Father,

I know that I have sinned and fallen short of Your expectations of me. I have come to realize that I cannot run my own life. I do not want to continue the way I've been living, neither do I want to face an eternity of torment and damnation.

I know that the wages of sin is death, but I can be spared from this through the gift of the Lord Jesus Christ. I believe that He died for me, and I receive His provision now. I will not be ashamed of Him, and I will tell all my friends and family members that I have made this wonderful decision.

Dear Lord Jesus,

Come into my heart now and live in me and be my Savior, Master, and Lord. I will do my very best to chase after You and to learn Your ways by submitting to a pastor, reading my Bible, going to a church that preaches about You, and keeping sin out of my life.

I also ask You to give me the power to be healed from any sickness and disease and to deliver me from those things that have me bound.

I love You and thank You for having me, and I am eagerly looking forward to a long, beautiful relationship with You.

Books by Mark T. Barclay

Beware of Seducing Spirits

This is not a book on demonology. It is a book about the misbehavior of men and women and the seducing and deceiving spirits that influence them to do what they do. Brother Barclay exposes the most prominent seducing spirits of the last days.

Beware of the Sin of Familiarity

This book is a scriptural study on the most devastating sin in the Body of Christ today. The truths in this book will make you aware of this excess familiarity and reveal to you some counterattacks.

Building a Supernatural Church

A guide to pioneering, organizing, and establishing a new local church. This is a fast-reading, simple, instructional guide to leaders and helps people who are working together to build the Church.

Charging the Year 2000

This book will remind you of the last-days' promises of God as well as alert you to the many snares and falsehoods with which satan will try to deceive and seduce last-days' believers. "A handbook for living in the '90s."

Enduring Hardness

God has called His Church an army and the believers soldiers. It is mandatory that all Christians endure hardness as good soldiers of Jesus Christ. This book will help build more backbone in you.

How to Avoid Shipwreck

A book of preventive medicine, helping people stay strong and full of faith. You will be strengthened by this book as you learn how to anchor your soul.

How to Relate to Your Pastor

It is very important in these last days that God's people understand the office of pastor. As we put into practice these principles, the Church will grow in numbers and also increase its vision for the world.

How to Always Reap a Harvest

In this book Brother Barclay explains the principles that make believers successful and fruitful. It shows you how to live a better life and become far more productive and enjoy a full harvest.

Improving Your Performance

Every Christian everywhere needs to read this book. Even leaders will be challenged by this writing. It will help tremendously in the organization and unity of your ministry and working force.

The Making of a Man of God

In this book you'll find some of the greatest, yet simplest, insights to becoming a man or woman of God and to launching your ministry with accuracy and credibility. The longevity of your ministry will be enhanced by the truths herein. You will learn the difference between being a convert, an epistle, a disciple, and a minister.

Preachers of Righteousness

This is not a book for pulpiteers or reverends only but for all of us. It reveals the real ministry style of Jesus Christ and the sold-out commitment of His followers— the most powerful, awesome force on the face of the earth.

The Real Truth About Tithing
This book is a thorough study of God's Word on tithing, which will fully inform believers how to tithe biblically and accurately. You will be armed with the truth, and your life will never be the same!

The Remnant Church
God has always had a people and will always have a people. Brother Barclay speaks of the upcoming revival and how we can be those who are alive and remain when our Master returns.

Sheep, Goats, Wolves
A scriptural yet practical explanation of human behavior in our local churches and how church leaders and members can deal with each other. You will especially enjoy the tests that are in the back of this book.

Six Ways to Check Your Leadings
It seems that staying in the main flow of Jesus is one of the most difficult things for believers to do, and I'm including some preachers. Many people border on mysticism and a world of fantasy. God is not a goofy god. He doesn't intend for His people to be goofy either. This book reveals the six most valuable New Testament ways to live in accuracy and stay perfectly on course. This book is a must for living in the '90s.

The Sin of Lawlessness
Lawlessness always challenges authority and ultimately is designed to hurt people. This book will convict those who are in lawlessness and warn those who could be future victims. It will help your life and straighten your walk with Him.

Warring Mental Warfare
Every person is made up of body, soul, and spirit and fights battles on each of these three fronts. The war against your soul (made up of your mind, will, and emotions) is real and as lethal as spiritual and natural enemies. This book will help you identify, war against, and defeat the enemies of your soul. Learn to quit coping with depression, anxiety, fear, and other hurts and begin conquering them now!

What About Death
This book deals with the enemy, death, and how to overcome it. I also explain what the Bible says about life after death. I have found that many people have no real biblical knowledge on this subject and therefore are unsure about it all the days of their lives.

Basic Christian Handbook (mini book)
This mini book is packed full of scriptures and basic information needed for a solid Christian foundation. It would make an inexpensive and effective tract and is a must for new converts. Many church workers are using it for altar counseling.

The Captain's Mantle (mini book)
Something happened in the cave Adullum. Find out how 400 distressed, indebted, and discontented men came out of that cave as one of the most awesome armies in history.

Have You Seen This Person Lately? (mini book)
Did you once serve the Lord actively and fervently but now you have cooled off some? Are you now serving Him and want to assure that you will never backslide? Do you have family or friends who are backslidden or unchurched? Then this book is for you! Its contents will help you find your way home.